Spiral To L;VE

Ta'Shayna Stinson

Presentation by *BookLeaf Publishing*

Web: www.bookleafpub.com

E-mail: info@bookleafpub.com

ISBN: 9789357211666

First edition 2023

Masquerade

You should see how different I am.
I am more different than most people I know.
I am more different than all the Definitions of
"Different" combined in a dictionary.
I am half Island and half mountains, even
islanders and mountain climbers wouldn't
understand me.
I am very deserted and shut off, looking within
myself for escape.
Unlike so many self photographers who snap
self-image shots .. I am a portrait and not an
un-detailed photo.
I am shade, very hidden unlike those that are
sunshine very revealing.
I am a blooming flower in winter when everyone
hibernates until next season.
I am a Queen on a Throne when others settle for
being a stoop .
I refuse to settle .
I won't settle, I am higher power who is Enough.
I am who used to be a memory, I will forever
exalt instead of fading.
I am the lyrics in my own paragraph.
I am the Swan in the industry and not the
Pigeon.

In Life, I am the Game refusing to be someone
else's game piece or property.
The person of Reality and not a character in their
untold story.
In Greek Mythology, I am my own Athena to all
the want to be Aphrodites.
I am the Mirror Reflection of Imperfection .
I am Different .. See ?

Third Person

Teeth glistening on her round brown face
Lips turned upside down
Her smile is a facade, the laugh just as well
She covers her feelings so no one can tell
But, look into her eyes and stare deep
Theres that pain you shall see
Her heart is aching, its throbbing with sorrow
She's giving up hope, the thought of tomorrow
Shes fighting the battles, tossing and turning
She takes Trazodone for a peaceful sleep
She wants to be alone but the emotions inside
run high, feelings are deep
No matter how hard she tries, when no one is
looking she seems to break down and cry
She won't dare tell
She feels its better to hide
The act she puts on everything is okay, No one
questions her its better that way
Great at pretending, its what they don't know
It seems something wont let go
Its not better to let her be, but the help she
receives from therapy will help her cope with
reality.

Eye For An Eye

I'm the one that will never be defined
I will not allow you to define me
I am the Rainbow unleashing in the storm
Is it a dream or a nightmare ?
Is it real ? Why can't it be concealed ?
The eyes are our natural revelance
The eye nerve is the spike of it all
Stuck in between lines while running out of time
The eyes tell a story
So tell it, speak now
A wild crowd ending in a bow
Wait free yourself and make a change flap your
lashes and like a butterfly spread your wings, its
time for you to fly.
The type of prisoner that has been captured
Words left unsaid locked away in my head
Silence .
Your eyes .
Eye for an Eye
I see you , may not belong but I need you .
Tears for that eye to cry, tired of unspoken lies
Hi's and goodbyes ending with sighs.
Eye for an Eye
I love you
Im not deranged but, trust I have changed

God created you and I
Like I said before We are a Rainbows cry .
Dark clouds is approaching
Too much to take in
Silence.
Speak up.
Eye for an Eye
Can you see me ?
Do you believe me ?
Far from perfect , emotions have surfaced
Eyes tell stories too, they cry and boo-hoo just
like we do.

Unwanted Guess

Who am I ?
I am a human becoming a soul
I am life in its physical formation
I myself am my own creation
You are unwanted salt in my ocean
The dangerous species in my sea
The shark so deadly , that stays chasing after me.
You are the quick sand I sink into
The crab ready to defend
Ready to take my heart in your claws
But, I wear a coat of protection
Because, I drink you in like water ..
I'll sweat you out the same
Forget the way your lips felt and eventually the
sound of your name .

Shattered Image

I want a love letter,
A letter of spoken words that tells me how
beautiful I am.
Tell me how my smile illuminates the room
Give me cofidence with my love handles
Tell me my body sets the mood and my eyes are
exotic.
A letter of how the hairs on my skin will rise at
every single touch.
Tell me im intelligent enough to comprehend
Show me flaws
A letter that will signal my appreciation of my
body
Forgive me for the pain I have caused you
Your body is a temple, it is a muse.
The mockery
The mirror mocks my every move, everything I
try to smooth
I want a love letter to hide my shyness
Speak to me, tell me dont be ashamed
Body changes are normal
Every reason to be hormonal
To be happy in your skin, soceity screams
perfection
Tell me in the letter to love me .

I want a love letter that screams you are your
creation
I'll never compete or compare
I am perfect in my own way .
From my lips ..
down to my hips ..
wondering to my toes ..
carressing every inch of me ..
I am perfect .
I want a love letter
Tell me stop looking deep into my shattered
reflection
The reflection is not me .
The glass shatters
The letter beside it
The pen in my hand
I want a love letter that describes my uniqueness
A letter of acceptance
Growth .
Change .
Age .
I am my love letter .
My body is a temple , it is my muse .

Skin

Ive been at war with myself
A battle itself ..
My battle scars are skin deep
Each tattoo covers the lining
My skin covers the scar tissue
The cries in each dark corner, where nobody
goes
Where nobody follows
The clicking sound of the locking of the door
Underneath her clothes plenty of sores
Years, upon years of letting them win
Not sure if this is making her sin
The scars of her past, all hidden so well
Shes pulled back in her shell
She's a master of disguise
You can see it now just look into her eyes ..
Sometimes people look and stare even ask
questions if they may
I just never knew what to say
It felt good for the moment
Then drained the life out of me .
Why can't you see what cutting was doing to me
I felt ashamed for submitting so easily
My mind in frantic ..
While trying not to panic .

Stains on my clothing
The clock ticking on the wall
Meanwhile im trying to make sense of it all .
Skin to Skin
People will always pick
I'll choose my pick to abuse .
Thighs, legs, arms
I sure did pick the place for demise
Nobody will ever know .
My tattoos cover them all .
Over and Under
I'll pick and choose, Nobody will know
Unless Im willing to show

His Addiction

The first time I seen you take your first hit ,
never knew what it meant .
The first time you gazed into its eyes
You was the beast of all highs .
The first time you kissed it I bet it reminded you
of the sweet alcohol
I know you felt the arousal of being lit
But why you couldn't just chill a bit ?
I know the feeling of pure bliss, it was written
all over your face how could it miss ?
The memories you and your addiction share
Is your wife and kids despair ..
Its the drug that took over
My mind was insane
Nothing but you and the drug that I blame .

Breathe ;

The sirens are closer than ever
The feeling I feel is anxious .
I'm alone .
Im dying .
I can't breathe .
My chest hurts, my head hurts, everything hurts .
Blood pressure rising , tempature increasing
Everything is at a stand still .
My head is spinning
Where am I ?
The sirens are approaching , in the air im lifted
Am I on a strecher ?
Its rollng .. Im moving.
Oh no ouch my chest hurts real bad
Im sad
Im faint in and out
The monitors are beeping
IV's all in my arms
Nurses in and out
I'm alone ..
The feeling won't go away
It's happening again
My body runs hot but somehow i'm cold
Its eating aways my insides strong , I just know
this is wrong .

My eyes are teary and my body is weak
To out of it to speak
My head is heavy which is very scary
Here comes the black outs and the nurses in and
out
I just wanna breathe and be okay
Somebody please hear me out .
Im screaming get these needles out of me I just
need to go
Here comes a nurse bringing me Lexapro
To weak to fight
Outta mind outta sight .
11:11 strikes the clock
Here the nurse is putting on addmiting socks .
Now im stuck in a hospital bed
Glad that im not dead
So what I shall say
I lived to fight my anxiety a whole nother day .

Disgusted

I dated you
You was my boo ..
Everything we did , we did it as one .
I thought the love was real
It was just a painful deal
It started off all good
You then told me you were misunderstood
The arguments down to the fights
You left me scared
Bruises left and right .
I just wanted you out of my sight
Where did it all begin , just ready for it to end
I walk away and you follow
The fear of not seeing my people tomorrow
Can't you see your hurting me ?
The two lines show on that test
I'm trying my best
Not to cry
Every single sigh
Pregnant with your seed you inflicted pain
indeed
Luckily the pregnacy ended naturally
I couldn't dare have your son
That means you wouldv'e won
I could never inflict pain upon a daughter

How would you treat her ?
Hell no not like me you see ?
I thought it was love
But it was just romantic "songs"
It started off great
I was your bait
You reeled me in
For that I left and didn't let you win .

Shitty Flowers

I hate flowers
I use to enjoy them
He took the life from that
Sunflowers, roses, dasiys , to a bouquet of
flowers
You name it
He use throw the flowers to me in bed
Rember don't bring me flowers when i'm dead
You stood tall
Made me feel so small
You stole my voice away and made me afraid to
speak .
I spoke my truth
I wouldn't dare apologize for being me
Somehow you won't let me be
Keep your shitty flowers
I had the marks
The bruises
All the makeup that drenches my body
You blamed me for every action
Every action doesnt need a reaction
I sit , you hit
I found myself fracturing beneath his fists
Beauty beaten in hues of purple, red, blue, and
yellow

Fresh
My body is my landscape
In which you roamed
I hate your shitty flowers
No apologies will make me forgive
No court orders will make stay
In my own world is where I will lay
Each bruise has become a battleshield
Every sore bone has healed
I'll give myself flowers standing strong
Its no more pretends, smiles, shame, and lies
No more ifs, maybes, or even whys ..
I am not your possession to abuse and keep .
Like a parasite you tried to consome my life
As a human being I tried to be lover and a
potential wife
Your guilt will eat you alive
But I still wish you best
Your pathetic and cruel
But its okay I kept my cool
I accepted my own flowers bloomng brightly
and strong .

Overcoming

I am a Survivor
I will not be a viction
You will not show me pity
You will not sit around me and cry
We will not be victimized
He did it once and could do it again
I will not allow
Trusting men is hard to do
When I tried to fight and couldn't sue ..
You took my body and made it your amour
It was by force and never rehearsed .
Upset for denying you
You did what you wanted
I was exhausted
Tired of fighting and screaming NO
They watched and listened and did nothing but
GO
How am I suppose to feel ?
My body you can't just steal .
I was vulnerable and you took advantage
To someone I put trust in
How could you?
You didn't make me feel safe
Instead you invaded my space ..
My privacy no more

I was so cold
You so bold
I am not your meat but you mad me a seat .
Sitting by the water
Ready to dive
Realizing I am at peace now
I am AL;VE

999 - Release

Numerology ..
Angel Number 999 is the sign of Release
I will as I please
I love my skin
I get creative with it
The outcome will be worth it
The pain is bearable
The pinch is just a sting
One , Two , Three
Its all done .
Nice and piereced up
Thats wassup
Your body is a work of art
So just pick the part
Tattoo needles I crave
Whew your very brave
My tattoos tell a story
Its my journey .
Life is a tattoo it comes in many shapes and
forms
All of us are marked .
The colors so vibrant so vivid im amused
So ink out my flesh
The sounds turn me on
It does something to me

Everything inked is my reminder
Its my release , my peace .
Haikus are stanzas of three lines
Let that ink bleed past the edges
Let it last forever
Cover me in tattoos,
Piercings galore
Confidence embrace
Without it your a bore .
Its my release, my peace.

Grief

They say death isn't easy .
They say to prepare for it
They say be ready for it
So you mean to tell me I'm suppose to be okay
Okay with you not comng back ..
These tears pile up on my pillow
Im very mellow
Calm and numb to it all
Picking up pieces to not fall
Gathering and processing my thoughts
Wondering hard
I pray you fought
I hope who did this gets caught .
Im empty .
No need for sympathy .
Empathy maybe .
My lucky number seven
I hope to see you in Heaven
Tears won't bring you back
I cried .
Words won't bring you back
I tried.
Just continue to look down from above
& Shower us with love .
I'll forever remember you far or near

I will never let you go my dear .
Get your rest
I'll see you soon
I love you all the way to the moon .

Future Grad

I see the confidence
I see the discussion boards
I see my grades
I'm shy and timid
Their acts are wealthy
Me being a social ilite is healthy
Not to extreme
I will climb to the top for my Degree
Life is strange with its twist and turns
But I continue to learn
Success is failure in and out
I will not doubt
The funds are low and the debts run high
All I do is sigh
I push forward and Breathe
Chapter after chapter I must read
I will keep saying I must succeed
When it becomes to much a bit
999 Release, Rest but, you must not quit

Ending ;

You matter
You must know your worth
You must say you are enough
I will not apologize for not feeling okay
If anything people made me this way
I wanted it to end
Just one break and a bend
I was ready to go
Wanted no one to know
I could see the devestation that I would leave
behind
That is what changed my mind
I couldve left without a warning
Leaving nothing but questions
I did believe I was facing this world alone
They sware they wouldve helped if they would
have known
How long have you been hurting ?
Deciding I was done
Your pain would have just begun ..
The moment I wouldve took my life
Yours wouldve ended too
I turned back time
And woke up
Realizing I wont be stuck

I'll go seek help
I'll be okay
I'll be here and wont leave without a fight
Push and Pull with all my might .
I'm here to stay , I have a story to tell
Hopefully this book sells .

Free

27

I am free
Free of everything
Free from my mind
Free from my soul
Free from my body
I am letting go
I am a Butterfly
I will fly .

Lost Files

I see you writing and joting your notes
I was afraid to be with you
I told you my problems and opened up to you
My Therapist
I put my trust in you
A sweet silence
In that silence, I examined the entire room
Each week, I sat in the corner of your couch
with damp tissue
You rocked in your chair
You listened
You cared
You knew me
You learned every part of me
For that I'm grateful ..
I thought you knew what I was going to say
Each in every way
My interior motives written in code .
You were there for my battles
When I felt I had no one
You was that someone
Every session worth every penny ..
Your not like many
I'll keep you close
You help me, I help you
It was great meeting you Sue .

Heal .

Young one,
Strong one,
Tough one,
You will survive your triumphs .
You will choose yourself
You must stand up
I will overcome those hidden wounds
Life must go on
Start healing your broken heart

www.ingramcontent.com/pod-product-compliance
Lightning Source LLC
LaVergne TN
LVHW021353200726
843509LV00014B/2818